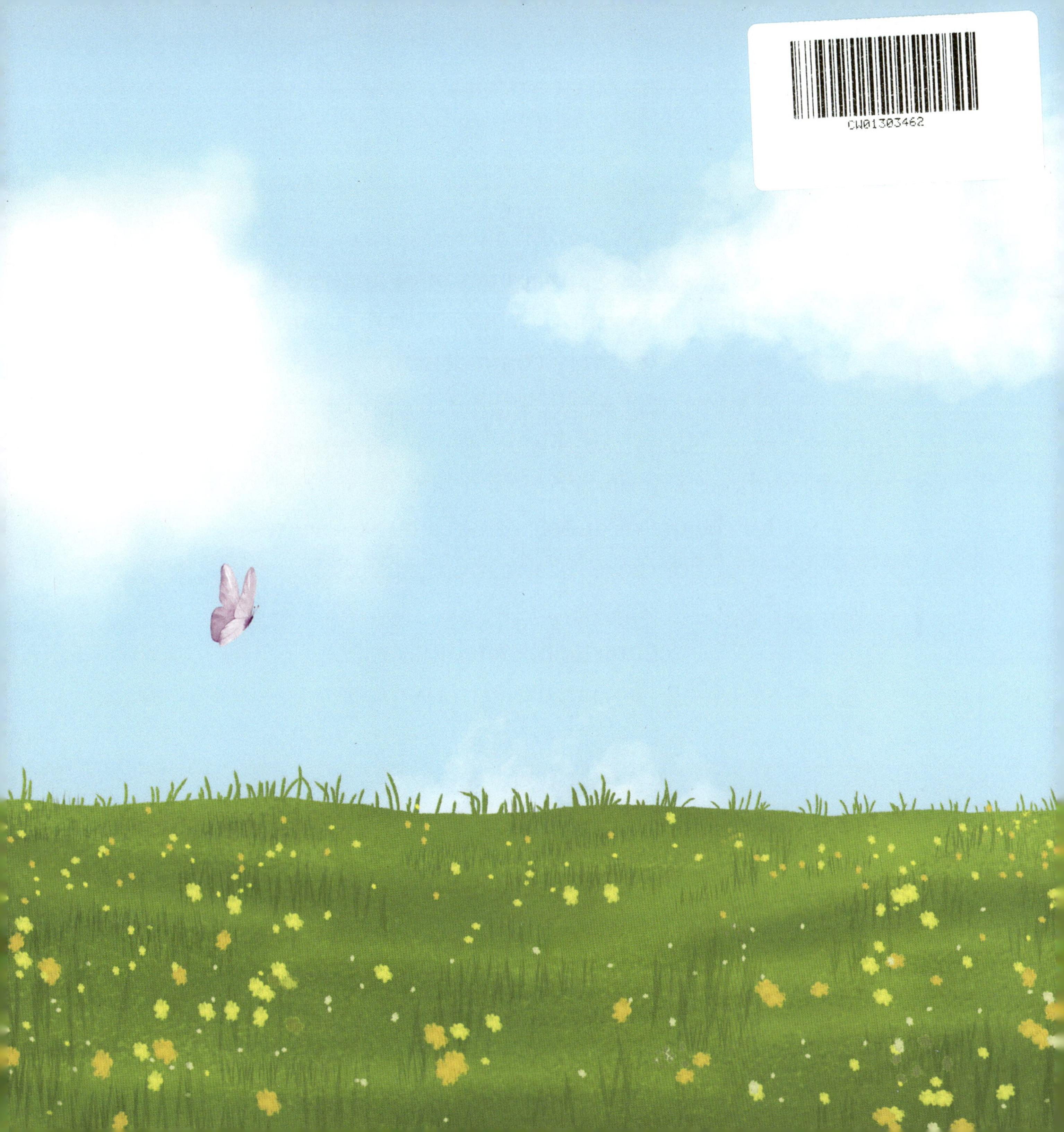

This is a work of fiction. Names, characters, places, and incidents either are the product of the author's imagination or are used fictitiously. Any resemblance to actual persons, living or dead, events, or locales is entirely coincidental.

Copyright © 2024 Liberated to Learn

All rights reserved. No part of this book may be reproduced or used in any manner without written permission of the copyright owner except for the use of quotations in a book review.

For more information, address:

contact@liberatedtolearn
liberatedtolearn.com

Liberated
TO
LEARN

A Home Educated Heart

For those who love to learn

I'm home educated.
Not everyone knows what that means.
But I often spend more time outside than looking at screens.

I'm free to roam the woods and all the places we go.
Sometimes we have routines,
and sometimes we go with the flow.

Some children go to school,
but school isn't right for me.
Instead I need an education that makes me feel free.

I'm not told what I should know — I learn what I like.
It may be something as simple as riding a bike.

I learn new things each and every day.
I'm not forced into anything and I do things my way.
I have choices to make and I take the lead.
But I also listen so that I will succeed.

A lack of routine — some people think it's crazy.
But my laidback schedule is far from lazy.
I'm on my feet the moment I open my eyes.
What the day will bring is a surprise.

Often people worry about how I make friends.
But Home Education doesn't mean that socialising ends.
Wherever I go, there's new people to meet.
It could be across the country or down the street.

I don't sit at home and watch TV for hours.
Yes, I like films but also learning about flowers.
I read books and play games. I do crafts and play sport.
There's nothing I can't do without the support.

Each day is a new experience, a treasured memory to make.
I do more than what most children do on their lunch break.

One day I learn how to cook. The next I sculpt some wood.
My childhood days never looked so good.

"**You should be in school.**"
It's the same phrase all the time.
But I've got better things to do and more trees to climb.

Behind four walls, who wants to be stuck in one room?
Get outside, watch the flowers bloom.

No one wants to be told what to do or how to learn.
It's time to take the reins and have your turn.

The world is my classroom. Have you heard that before?
Don't wait around, it's yours to explore!

I'm not stuck at a desk with a pen in my hand,
or forced to learn a subject I simply can't stand.
My schedule's my own, with endless time to explore.
I've learnt more than I ever have before.

Education is more than just textbooks and taking exams.
Why force children to follow all the same programmes?
We all learn differently. We're not the same.
I've always played a different game.

I can change my mind if I want to try school.
But then I'd be stuck with rule after rule.
For me, freedom is what matters most.
I love being home educated, but I won't boast.

Some people worry that they haven't got time to home educate.
Or that they've got way too much already on their plate.

But learning doesn't need to be planned or timed to perfection.
It can take you in any direction.

Whether it's half an hour or a whole day.
Learning is learning, and that's okay.
The value isn't in how much, it's *what* I learn.
Getting left behind is of no concern.

Everyone goes at their own pace and judgement is rare.
The community cares about everyone's welfare.

I still face challenges. No day is perfect you see.
But I try my best and stay carefree.
There are ups and downs, I will not lie.
But after you fall, the next time you'll fly.

I love learning at home, or wherever I go.
And the more I learn, the more I grow.

The future is bright, opportunities are wide.
And all the way, it's been a ride.

I wake up content and go to bed with a smile; knowing that no matter what I've done, it's been worthwhile.

I'm home educated.
Not everyone will understand.
But it's right for me, and the choice is grand.

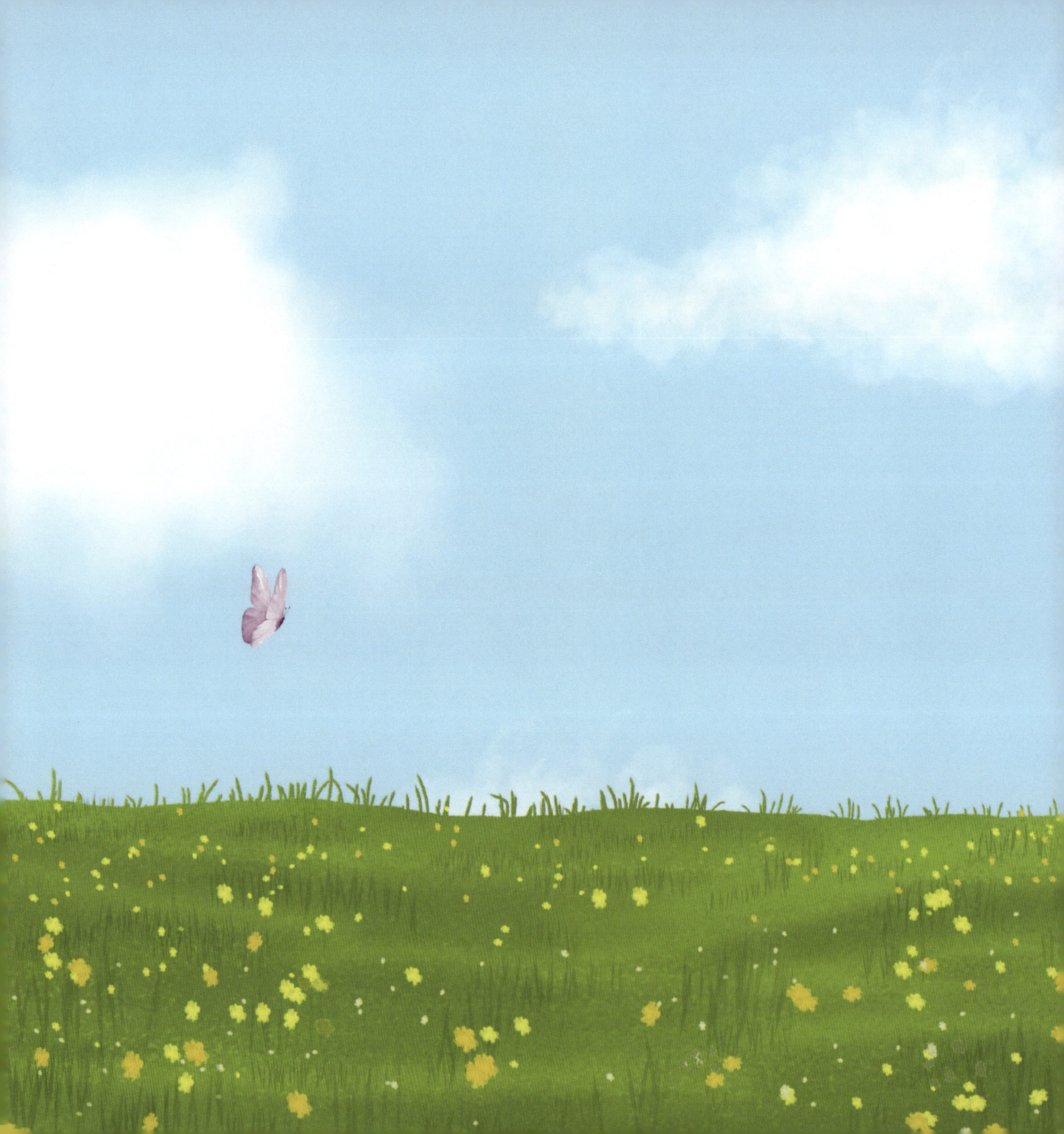

Printed in Great Britain
by Amazon